**RAND M^CNALLY**

S0-AZR-740

Swamps & Marshes

A *Where Are We?* Book

by Chris Arvetis
and Carole Palmer

illustrated by James and Doris Buckley

Rand McNally for Kids™
Books•Maps•Atlases

Swamps are found all over the world. Any area that is usually covered by water where trees and shrubs grow can be a swamp. The water is generally not more than three feet deep.

River-fed swamps have fresh water while ocean-fed swamps have salt water. The type of water determines the kinds of plants and animals that live there.

Yes!
This is a swamp in the lowlands by the ocean.
The land is covered by water most of the time.
The water comes from the ocean and is salt water.

River

Ocean

Plants adapt to the wet environment. Their roots stay near the surface in order to get oxygen from the air.

Bonnet lilies

Trees and shrubs grow everywhere.
Vines hang from the trees and moss grows on the tree trunks.
There are beautiful plants and lots of animals, too.

Swamp sunflowers

Marsh pinks

Naked ladies

A variety of animals live in the coastal swamps.

Cottonmouth
moccasin

Many different kinds of turtles
and frogs like the swampy water.
Lots of snakes crawl around.
Even alligators and crocodiles
live in some parts of this swamp.

Ribbit.

What's your name?

Alligator

Birds live here, too. Woodpeckers and warblers as well as special birds like flamingos, egrets, and herons like the swamp.

Unusual birds also live in the water and in the trees.

1 Flamingo
2 Woodpecker
3 Warbler
4 Great blue heron
5 Eagle

Blue heron

Hi!

White ibis

Mockingbird

Anhinga

One kind of swamp along tropical seacoasts is the mangrove swamp. It is named after the mangrove trees that grow here.
Snails, pelicans, monkeys, and many sea animals can be found. Parrots and egrets sit in the mangrove trees.

Many of the earth's tropical shores were once covered by mangrove trees. Some roots grow out of the trunk and branches to support the trees, and others hold the trees in the mud.

Water buffaloes live in the Australian mangrove swamps. Tigers are found in the mangrove swamps of Bangladesh and India.

1 Parrot
2 Monkey
3 Pelican
4 Snail
5 Egret

Tiger

Water buffalo

Swamps can be found along many of Africa's inland rivers. The heat and humidity make the swamps thick with plants. Papyrus grows out of the water, and water lilies and water cabbage float on the surface of the swamps.

Some big swamps are near rivers and have fresh water. These swamps can have lots of water or just a little depending on the rains.
Hardwood trees with vines and shrubs are everywhere.

Papyrus

Kingfisher

Hippopotamus

Marshes are another kind of land area covered by water. But no trees grow here. Marshes have grasses, cattails, rushes, and sedges.

Plants like grasses are found in marshes. Some of the plants have thick roots or stems that attach to the mud. Others float on the water.

Water soldier

Common sedge

Yellow water lily

Common reed

Bul

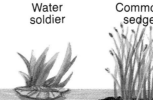

Birds of all kinds can be found in marshes. These wading birds search for food — eating insects, plants, or fish of the marshes.

Blackwinged stilt   Purple heron   Little egret

An estuary forms where a freshwater river runs into the saltwater ocean. In this water mixture, there are more varieties of life than other places on earth.

Saltwater marshes (tidal marshes) form in estuaries, on offshore sandbars, on islands, and on spits. Twice each day, the tide brings in the salt water and food to supply a feast for the herons, curlews, brown pelicans, bald eagles, and golden plovers.

1 Canadian geese
2 Mallard
3 Coot
4 Water rail

Ducks, turtles, snails, and frogs live among the grasses. Flowering plants make some marshes a beautiful sight. Water lilies float on the water. In some places, small water plants are so thick that the water looks green.

Another type of marsh is the delta marsh which forms at the mouth of a river. The Athabasca Delta in northern Canada attracts flocks of snow geese. Large bison, muskrats, and beavers live at the delta.

Beavers, muskrats, raccoons, mink, and land animals like bear and deer can be seen here.
The marsh hawk, teal, and red-wing blackbird are interesting birds that live here.

Bogs are another kind of land area covered with water. The water comes from rainfall. It makes the land wet and spongy. Only a few kinds of plants grow here — mainly mosses.

I like the color of this moss.

Bogs develop in shallow lakes, usually in areas where glaciers scooped out the land. Bogs are found in cool damp places. Sphagnum moss can be found in many bogs. It floats like a mat and absorbs water like a sponge.

Cranberry bog

Sphagnum moss

Lots of berries grow here!
Cranberry, bunchberry, and
blueberry bushes like the
wet, soggy bog.
Bogs are well-known for peat
moss, which forms peat.
Peat is made of dying plants that
pile up in layers in the water.

Peat can be found under the layer of moss. Peat is formed when decayed plants pile up in layers at the bottom of the pond. The peat is harvested and burned to make electricity in some countries. Peat is also harvested and added to soil because it holds water.

Lots of bugs — mosquitoes, beetles, and dragonflies — live in the bogs. A few birds like owls, hawks, and warblers can also be seen. Bog turtles, otters, mink, and bog lemmings live here, too.

1 Owl
2 Weasel
3 Marsh wren
4 Caddis fly
5 Damselfly
6 Marsh hawk
7 Mosquito
8 Dragonfly
9 Pondskater
10 Whirligig beetle

Bogs have become famous for discoveries that have provided clues to the past.

A fen is a type of bog. It has grasslike plants, grasses, sedges, reeds, and a few trees. Fens are found in areas that were once covered by glaciers. Unusual flowers and some well-known animals live here.

Black spruce

A *fen* is similar to a bog, but it usually gets its water from an underground spring. The main plants in a fen are sedges, grasses, and reeds. Peat is also found here.

Venus's flytrap

Snowshoe hare

Moose

Swamps, marshes, bogs, and fens are *wetlands*.

Wetlands help control floods and help stop soil erosion.

In many places, wetlands have been drained and destroyed.

Now people are working to save the wetlands — homes for birds, fish, and animals and beautiful areas for people to enjoy.

Wetlands are land areas where the water level is near or above the ground. Swamps, marshes, bogs, and fens are the major types of wetlands. Look at the wetland areas in the diagram.

Water table   High water   Low water   Water table   High water   Low water   Stream   River   Water table

Wetlands were once thought of as waste land and many were drained or destroyed. Now people have become aware of the value of the wetlands and have started programs to save them.